OUTRAGEOUS
FIBS WE TEL
THE KIDS

OUTRAGEOUS FIBS WE TELL THE KIDS

Darling, the ice-cream van only plays music when it's run out of ice cream.

The Best Lies Grown-Ups Tell Children

Charlie Ellis

Sure, kids are adorable, squishy-faced little darlings, but sometimes you really want them to get up, quiet down, consume something healthy or generally be on their best behavior. And, as we all know, that's what hardcore bribery and lying are for. Some lies just slip out: "You won't feel a thing," "It's past your bedtime," or "You can do anything you set your mind to." Others require a bit of clever crafting to get the required result.

This is the ultimate collection of big-person prevarications, including heaps of falsehoods to try out on the little people in your life—to stop them from peeing in the pool or to make them cut soda out of their diets. Plus, there are reams of real-life red herrings that other irresponsible adults have spun to excellent effect.

If you've ever told a child that Santa is real, you're already well on your way to mastering the art of deception. Whether you're fine with fibs or only need the occasional departure from the truth, one thing ain't no lie: you love those mini monsters and all the chaos that comes with them.

We grew up in the countryside, quite far from friends' houses. My parents told us that the TV only worked when it rained. We were always outside playing because we thought there were no other options. It was almost a treat when the heavens opened because it meant we got to turn the TV on. I'm not sure it would work on kids today, but it might be worth a try!

HOW TO MANAGE YOUR KIDS' INTERNET ADDICTION

Blame the government. Tell them there's a new national policy of rationing the internet so it doesn't run out. Shut-down time for kids under 12 is 8 p.m. Turn your router off around this time until they nod off, and then turn it back on so you can catch up on your Instagram feed.

HOW TO DRINK GUILT-FREE

Parenting is HARD WORK. Moms and dads often need a little time out with a beer or glass of wine. To make sure you can enjoy yours in peace, tell your inquisitive brood that adults drink [insert tipple of choice here] because it's special brain medicine for older people. For the medicinal effects to be felt, it needs to be taken in silence.

These days, kids have seen EVERYTHING and know EVERYTHING else. If you're having trouble impressing yours, try convincing them something isn't real. Tell them zebras are like unicorns, or elephants are like dinosaurs—magical or extinct. Then, take them to the zoo or out on safari, and pretend that you're all seeing this fascinating creature for the first time.

HA HA HA

"

My daughter used to throw a tantrum every time we had to leave the park. I told her that only when all the humans leave can the squirrels and rabbits come out of hiding to play on the slide and take over the swings. Now, as soon as it's time to leave she starts yelling at all the other kids to get the hell out of there so the squirrels can play too.

"

Children are to buttons as are moths to a flame. If you don't want them to touch it, make sure the consequence for doing so is pretty dire. The flight attendant call button on a plane? It opens the trapdoor beneath your feet and parachutes you back home. The hazard warning button in the car? It ejects you out of your seat and notifies the SWAT team of an imminent attack.

HOW TO GET THEM TO TAKE A LONG WALK

Inspire some hiking enthusiasm by letting them in on this nugget: if you don't use your child feet enough, they'll turn into hands, and then you'll be all wobbly when you try to walk. And they don't make Nikes for hands.

Getting kids to finish up their food, especially if it's something they're not that keen on, can be a right pain. We could never get my son to eat enough. Then we told him that every grain of rice left in his bowl equalled a year of bad luck. Now he scrapes the bowl clean and sometimes asks for more—I think he reckons the more rice he eats the more good luck he'll have. Who am I to argue?

HOW TO MAKE SURE THEIR COMPLAINTS ARE HEARD

Preschoolers have lots of complaints for such tiny people. To make sure they feel like you're taking their bawling seriously, buy an old phone and pretend to plug it in. Tell your toddlers that if they pick it up and dial 7, they'll get the national complaints answering service. They can then complain away to their heart's content.

When you're driving in the rain, tell your pint-sized passengers that you have magic powers and can make the rain stop for a second. Count down as you're about to go under a bridge or a tunnel, 3 ... 2 ... 1 ... and magically the rain disappears! On busy highways, this could keep them amused for hours.

HA HA HA

HOW TO MAKE INJECTIONS LESS SCARY

Going to the doctor for a shot is terrifying for the hardiest of adults, so it's understandable why kids get the jitters. Tell your kids that the most effective shots are delivered via a needle inserted directly into their eyes, but that you've phoned ahead to make sure they get the special non-eye injections instead. When you get there, they'll be rolling up their shirtsleeves with glee!

My mother told me not to put my finger in the electrical sockets because a tiny woman lived in there and she'd bite my finger off. I never went near them as a result, but when she told my brother, he became fascinated with the woman in the socket. He left her little notes and snacks, and would sit in front of the empty socket reading to her from his storybooks.

If your kids pester you to take them to a 12A or PG-13 movie that you'd rather they didn't see, tell them yes, but that they'd better hurry to the cinema because they only let 12 (or 13) people into those screenings. When you arrive, tell them it's already booked up and pick something more appropriate.

It might be too late for you, but make sure your children save themselves from scrolling comas by putting down their devices and getting outdoors. Tell them that after three hours of being indoors, they're breathing in all the air that other people have breathed out, filled with all their germs. Gross!

To make sure our two children weren't using tablets or torches to keep reading after lights out, we once told them that reading in the dark would damage their eyes. But we'd also told them that eating their carrots would help them see in the dark. One night, we heard giggling coming from their room and found the two of them hunkered under a duvet with torches, munching on carrot sticks which they'd sneaked from the fridge before bedtime.

If your child was born on a public holiday, such as Christmas or New Year's Day, they have to share their birthday with the celebrations. Rather than have them feeling second best, tell them the reason everyone in the country has the day off is to celebrate their special day!

HA HA HA

HOW TO KEEP THEM HYDRATED

Getting kiddos to drink enough water when they want juice, pop or milkshake can be tricky. Old people come in handy here. When you walk past a particularly wrinkly looking oldie, say to your children, "He's actually 12, but he didn't drink enough water when he was your age and his body dried up."

HOW TO GET THEM TO TURN OFF THE TV

Kids are past the days of believing that if they watch too much TV their eyes will turn square-shaped, but they might just be convinced by this corker. If they're glued to the box, tell them that the people in the TV will start to think they're auditioning and zap them into TV land, and that once they're there they won't be able to come home.

When my daughter was five I told her that if she could lick her own elbow she would miraculously turn into a boy. She wouldn't dare try it because the thought of being a boy terrified her. A couple of years later, when her baby brother was born, I noticed her licking his elbows a few times. When I quizzed her about it, she said 'I wanted a baby sister.'

If your kids think they've seen a ghost or are worried about ghouls coming for them in the night, you can let them in on a commonly known "fact": most people aren't rich enough to afford a ghost —that's why they're usually found in big creepy houses, not suburban semis.

HOW TO AVOID THE BATH BECOMING THE TOILET

While some environmentalists might argue in favor of a quick tinkle in the tub, you don't want your kid to be the one who makes a habit of it. This is why it makes good common sense to tell them that if they decide to relieve themselves while taking a shower, their urine will come out of the showerhead.

HA HA HA

"Oh look over there!" is a classic parent move to steal a chip off your kid's plate. I always tell mine about a story in the news about burgers being poisoned, so I have to taste-test theirs first EVERY TIME.

HOW TO CONVINCE THEM CAFFEINE'S NOT FOR KIDS

There's no denying you NEED your morning latte, but that doesn't mean you want to encourage caffeine addiction too young. Avoid them getting hooked on the good stuff by telling them caffeine has a special chemical reaction in kids' brains that makes their ears fall off. This works for alcohol too—that's why it's illegal for kids to buy it.

HOW TO BAN BURPING

"Better out than in" is a mantra most of us live by, but if you want your angelic heirs to behave themselves in public, tell them that burps are farts that have got confused and come out the wrong way. When they feel one coming, they should swallow it down so as not to fart on everyone at the dinner table. There's also the well-known fact that you'll never get invited to any posh parties if you get a reputation as a burper.

HOW TO STOP YOUR CHILD SUCKING THEIR THUMB

The age-old wisdom that your thumb will fall off if you continue to suck it usually does the trick, but if your special sucker is refusing to succumb to that one, how about telling them that you want to take them to [insert special fun thing here], but kids who suck their thumbs have been banned. It's the LAW.

My eldest son told his younger brother that if he sneezes with his eyes open, they'll pop right out of his head. The younger one is now so terrified of sneezing, when he feels a sneeze coming on, he sits on the floor and covers his eyes, just waiting for them to fall out.

HOW TO MAKE LONG JOURNEYS SEEM SHORTER

Road trippin' with toddlers can be a headache. Avoid incessant arguing and "Are we there yet?" whining with this sneaky bribe/lie. Tell them if they fall asleep, you'll take the shortcut and when they wake up, they'll nearly be there. Watch them nod off and enjoy the drive in peace.

HA HA HA

HOW TO WASTE LESS WATER

Kids are more environmentally conscious than ever, but that doesn't stop the little buggers brushing their teeth while leaving the tap running. Keep your water bills down by telling them a magical fish lives behind the mirror and the water comes straight from his supply. If they leave it running too long, poor Nemo will be floundering for his life.

I've always been convinced that kids would love vegetables if they thought they were special. With my own kids, I always left sweets and sugary treats lying around and told them they could eat as many as they wanted. The vegetables were locked away in a high cupboard and only eaten at dinner. It worked! My son asked for a bowl of carrots for his fifth birthday instead of a cake.

HOW TO GET YOUR FUSSY KIDS TO EAT

They might always be hungry, but when it comes to feeding youngsters something out of the ordinary (or just broccoli), they can turn their noses up in disgust. Don't let your diet suffer—tell them that different textures have different health benefits. So slimy foods help them swim faster, crunchy foods stop their teeth falling out, foods covered in sauce help them develop a waterproof layer of skin, and so on.

HOW TO PREVENT NOSE-PICKING

Curb this unsavory habit by telling your picking progeny that boogers are tiny pieces of their brain that have traveled to their nostrils. Every time they have a good rummage around and pick one out, they're making their brain smaller. They're getting dumber, one booger at a time.

Kids are scared of breaking the law. Exploit this if you can. For example, want the weeding done, stat? Tell your little helpers that growing dandelions (or whatever other pesty weeds you've got) is illegal—they'll be out there pulling them up and throwing them in the trash in no time. Want someone to pick up all the toys in the living room? Tell them the police are coming over for a toy inspection.

HA HA
HA HA

My little sister was very sensitive growing up and the first time she spotted a dead rabbit on the road our parents told her that it was taking a nap there because the road was really warm. I'm not sure she believed them, but from then on, she would joyously point out all the dead, flattened animals we passed on a family road trip with glee.

HOW TO MAKE THEM WANT A BATH

Practicing good personal hygiene is easy for adults, but kids need a bit of encouragement. Tell them if they don't take a bath, they'll start to smell like a dog. Apparently, smelling bad take years off your life—that's why one human year equals seven dog years.

Crossing the road safely is serious stuff, but make it more fun for kids by explaining that traffic lights and pedestrian crossings are fitted with high-tech cameras. Children who cross safely earn government points, which they can trade in for cool prizes when they turn eighteen. Children who behave badly at the roadside are forced to clean the oil stains from the tarmac. You can't argue with government policy.

When my five-year-old asked me why I loved broccoli so much, I told her that the more vegetables you eat the more they start to taste like candy. So after eating broccoli every week for 32 years it tasted sooooo good. She insisted on eating broccoli every night for two weeks after that.

HOW TO PHONE IN SOME BACKUP

When you're trying to get kids to toe the line, it helps to have another responsible adult around to enforce what you've said. But how about blaming decisions on the big man upstairs? Tell your kids that the asterisk symbol on the phone is a direct line to heaven. Call "God" (or Santa, if preferred), and ask him for a final ruling on any domestic discussions. Remember though, only adults are allowed to speak to God/Santa.

HOW TO STOP KIDS LEAVING THE FRIDGE OPEN

Tell them each fridge is powered by the South Pole and that there is a special penguin guardian installed behind it. If you leave the fridge open too long, the penguin will overheat and get ill, and then you'll be banned from owning a fridge by South Pole authorities.

HA HA HA

HOW TO HAVE A HEALTHY MEAL OUT

It can be hard to avoid unhealthy foods, especially when you're eating out and the kids can read the menu. Try telling them French fries are only for French people, hot dogs are only for warm canines and shakes are only for sheikhs. Sadly, they can't have any of those.

My youngest son was acting up at school, so I told him that parents had a special TV channel they could watch during the day to check up on how their kids were behaving. For a week I asked his teacher to tell me what he'd been up to. When I picked him up, I told him about what I'd "watched." He was soon on his best behavior in class!

HOW TO EXPLAIN WHERE BABIES COME FROM

Everyone knows you buy babies at hospitals. The only reason Mom gets really fat is because she's been eating more than usual to prove to the hospital that the family has enough money to have a baby. Obviously.

HOW TO AVOID A FEAR OF SPIDERS

Even if you're terrified of eight-legged critters, don't let your children grow up with the same irrational fear. Tell them that spiders live in an underground world where they worship human giants as their deities. When you see a spider, it's not come to scare you—far from it—it's come on a pilgrimage to pay its respects. Best thing to do is thank it for its devotion and ask it politely if it needs a lift to the nearest window so it can get back to its home!

When my brother and I were kids, our dad told us that we had to be silent when the turn signal was on because the other drivers needed to be able to hear the clicking sound, and if they couldn't hear it, we might crash. Turns out it was just to shut us up when we were getting too boisterous.

HOW TO MAKE SPINACH SEEM SPECIAL

Spinach makes you strong, right? Encourage your kids to scoff down the stuff by telling them if they eat enough of it, they'll be able to lift the house. Halfway through dinner, or if appetites are waning, take them outside and get them to have a go at lifting the building. Yell out "I think it's moving! Quick, you need to eat more!" before running back inside to watch them finish with glee.

HA HA HA

HOW TO GET YOUR FAIR SHARE OF THE SWEETS

Use a cunning lie to enforce a strict rule when it comes to candy, e.g. all the brown M&Ms are for adults only or the last piece of chocolate bar legally belongs to the person who bought it.

HOW TO GET THEM TO WASH THEIR HANDS

Scare your kids into good hygiene habits by explaining that slugs are little children who didn't wash their hands—that's why they're always on the garden path or pavement, trying to find their way back home. Point them out on the walk to school and get your sparklingly clean kids to try to guess what they were like as humans.

I tell my brood that "Happy Meals" are for kids who behave well on their way to McDonald's and that there are these other "Sad Meals" for naughty kids that just include water and carrot sticks.

HOW TO TRICK THEM OUT OF REGULAR ICE CREAMS

The first time they hear the ice-cream truck coming with its familiar music blaring, tell them that if the music is playing it means they've run out of ice cream. Buy them the occasional ice cream from a stationary truck so they believe you even more.

HOW TO MAKE
SODA UNCOOL

It's bad for their teeth, and water is so much cheaper, but kids can't help pestering their parents for soda, especially when they see you drinking it. To turn your kids off the sugary stuff, tell them it's black water, which adults have to drink in order to save the good water for the kids.

HA HA HA

Nothing fights monsters quite like an unusual kitchen utensil. We told our son that the potato masher was a magic stick that terrified monsters, and tucked it in with him at night. We also put the blender in his bedroom when he was really scared. We told him it was like a Venus flytrap for monsters, and the next day we blended them into a green smoothie.

HOW TO GET YOUR KIDS TO BELIEVE IN ALIENS

Tell them that lightning storms happen when our planet is warring with another one. If they believe aliens are real you can use this excuse to make sure they do what you want, e.g. "Put your toys away because an alien battle is expected tonight and we need to be ready."

HOW TO PUT AN END TO THEM PESTERING YOU FOR A DOG

Rather than saying no and being the bad guy, if your kids want a dog, tell them they have to prove they can look after a plant first. Buy them a plant and see how they do. They're bound to kill it anyway, but if you're feeling particularly mischievous, spray it with weed killer when they're not around. Give them as many chances as they can stand. They'll eventually admit defeat and stop pestering you.

HOW TO GET THEM TO PUT THEIR COATS ON

When it's raining, the last thing you want is your kids soaked to the bone. Make sure they grab their coats with glee before they leave the house by explaining that when it's raining, a scary sky giant is watering his garden. Rain jackets have a protective coating that makes you invisible to sky giants. Forget to wear one and he might think you're a garden pest and scoop you up in his trowel, never to be seen again.

I'm only 5 feet tall, so carrying my kids once they were toddlers was really hard. Exasperated one day, I told my oldest, who was nearly four, that I really wanted to carry him but that the doctor had told me his legs would stop growing if I did. I didn't think it would make a difference, but he refused to be carried for long after that.

HOW TO STOP THEM PICKING THINGS UP IN THE SUPERMARKET

Making your children aware of Big Brother early on will make sure they're on their best behavior in public. When you're browsing the aisles, remind them that they're being filmed and that if they're caught picking up things they can't afford, you'll get arrested in their place and thrown in prison FOREVER.

HA HA HA

HOW TO MAKE THEM AVID READERS

Want your offspring to be at the top of their reading game? If they struggle to sit down with a book, tell them reading is an essential brain function. If they don't practice enough it will lead to voice loss, tummy aches, and any other appropriate ailment. Coincide this with a sore throat or bout of diarrhea and they'll be bookworms in no time.

> My husband's family lives abroad, so we've had to take the kids on planes since they were babies. I'm always really embarrassed when they start screaming or yelling, so I told them that if they caused any problems on the flight out, they wouldn't be allowed on the flight back and we would have to leave them behind. If they caused problems on the flight back, I always said that the airline would put it on their file and ban them on the next trip.

A pacifier might have done the trick when you wanted them to settle in those early years, but no preschooler should be caught sucking on one. Wean them off by telling them the Pacifier Fairy only has a limited supply and now they're a big kid she needs to take it back to give to one of the new babies. You could even leave it in the garden for the Fairy to find.

Belly buttons can be used to answer lots of questions, especially when you don't know the answer (or don't want to discuss it). "Where do babies come out?" "Mommy's belly button." "What is a black hole?" "It's like your belly button for the universe." "I'm bored!" "Stare into your belly button for long enough and you'll discover a family of tiny gnomes living there..."

HOW TO KEEP THEM QUIET

Sometimes your kids are as cute as a litter of Labrador puppies in a sunflower field, but when your pups are yapping and whining, you wish they had a word limit per day, right? Now they do. Tell them that there's a chip in their brain that detects when they've reached a 10,000-word limit and that they won't be able to speak again if they go above it. They'll think long and hard before moaning about what's for dinner.

HA HA HA

Before I took my son for his first proper haircut, I asked the barber to play along and pretend he was going to cut my kid's ear off if he didn't sit still in the seat. He didn't wriggle once, but he did look terrified.

HOW TO ENJOY A KID-FREE NEW YEAR'S EVE

Little ones want to stay up to see in the new year, but it doesn't need to be the new year in the country they live. Show them the footage of celebrations in Sydney, turn the clocks forward, and send them off to bed at a reasonable hour for you to enjoy a few drinks in peace. Better yet, record last year's broadcast and play that instead.

HOW TO STOP YOUR KIDS FROM LYING (IRONIC, EH?)

While it's certainly a case of "do as I say, not as I do," tell your kids that when they lie their eyes will change color. When they tell a blatant lie, look shocked as you pretend you can see their eyes changing (try to do it before they can look in a mirror). If you're convincing enough, they'll soon stop that fearless fibbing.

Growing up we hardly ever had ice cream sundaes when we went out to eat. That's because my dad had my sister and I convinced that they were only available on Sundays. Conveniently, we rarely went out to eat on Sundays.

HOW TO KEEP ANNOYING TOYS TO A MINIMUM

When a well-meaning friend or family member buys your kid an impossibly irritating toy, don't let it rule your roost. Tell your child that they don't make replacement batteries for that particular toy, so when it runs out, it's done. They'll ration their usage to the point where you'll wonder if they even have it anymore. Ah, bliss!

HOW TO MAKE SURE TAKING THE GARBAGE CANS OUT

Taking out the trash is a chore, but your kid will be ready and willing if you tell them this: when the garbage collectors come round, if they see that you've not put out all your garbage, they'll snatch a child to put in the truck instead.

HA HA HA

> Me and my sister were always really well behaved when we went clothes shopping. That's because my mom told us that the child mannequins were children who had misbehaved and had been cursed by the store manager. I'm still a bit freaked out by store mannequins.

HOW TO NEVER HAVE TO LISTEN TO CRACKING KNUCKLES AGAIN

Like chalk on a blackboard, knuckle cracking probably sends a cold shiver down your spine. Tell your double-jointed darling that cracking knuckles causes arthritis, or worse, paralysis. They'll soon think twice before playing the glockenspiel on their digits.

HOW TO MAKE SURE THEY PLAY NICE, EVEN WHEN YOU'RE NOT IN THE ROOM

They might be angels when you're close by, but sibling sass probably breaks out as soon as you've turned your back. Try telling them that the smoke detectors are Santa cameras with a live feed to the North Pole. Naughty behavior should be swiftly replaced by nothing but nice.

We had a bit of trouble toilet-training our youngest. He would go to the bathroom but would forget to wipe his butt. We told him that if he didn't clean up after using the toilet, eventually his butthole would close up and he'd have to poop out of his mouth instead. Disgusting, but effective.

HOW TO STOP YOUR KIDS FROM PEEING IN THE POOL

Peeing in the sea is fine, right? But no one wants to take a dip in a pool filled with urine. So, for the sake of the other swimmers, and to make sure your little one doesn't wait till it's too late, tell them the pool has a special chemical in it that turns pee bright red. They'll be rushing to the bathroom to be spared the humiliation.

HOW TO EXPLAIN WHAT YOU WERE DOING IN THE BEDROOM

Locking the door is the obvious solution here. But if your kids *do* find you and your partner in a compromising situation, and they're too young to understand what was actually going on, tell them you were playing Twister in bed, or that you were giving each other a relaxing massage. Alternatively, explain that you were trying out a new form of couples' aerobics that you learned at the gym.

We filmed our daughter's birth. When she was six and going through a naughty phase, we played it to her in reverse and told her that if she continued to misbehave that's what would happen to her. We also incorporated our "where do babies come from" talk into the same terrifying session.

HOW TO MAKE HOSPITALS LESS SCARY

Going for an op or having to see the doctor can be daunting. Tell kids that hospitals are where all the world's fairies are born to make sure the trip is filled with anticipation instead of dread. In fact, nurses and doctors are actually magical fairy apprentices who have to spend a year living as humans and doing good deeds before they get promoted to full fairy status.

HOW TO SHARE AND SHARE ALIKE

Keep whining to a minimum by explaining that all toys are rented from the country's national toy library, even the ones in toy shops. That means they don't belong to anyone and should be shared. Kids who don't share have their toy library card revoked, their name put on a blacklist, and face a penalty where they won't be able to play with any new toys for a month.

Living out in the countryside, my sister and I would often go berry picking in the summer. To stop us picking unripe ones, mom told us that green berries were ones that had been peed on by dogs. She had a tough job getting us to eat green apples, yellow plums and kiwi fruits after that.

HOW TO GET THEM TO RESPECT THEIR ELDERS

Whether it's Grandma and Grandpa or the grumpy old man next door, you probably want your kids to be polite to the elderly. Convince your children that everyone over the age of 60 lived through some kind of zombie apocalypse or "end of the world" scenario. That way they'll be fascinated to hear their stories and more understanding when they're super-slow or a little bit grouchy.

Stretch the truth to your advantage by telling your environmentally conscious kids that not making their bed is bad for the environment (carbon they emitted during their sleep will escape from the sheets); that opening cans of pop releases toxic chemicals into the atmosphere; and that spitting toothpaste into the sink regularly keeps the water supply healthy.

HA HA HA

HOW TO KEEP THEM CLOSE

Losing your kids in a sea of people is terrifying. Make sure yours stick to you like glue by telling them about crowd clowns—undercover demons who wait for children to wander off and then snatch them and take them to their underground lair. Soon they'll be filled with fear and holding your hand for all they're worth.

Whenever someone farts, I can't help but think of what my grandpa told me as a kid: a fart is two turds whispering to each other. When I was younger I used to try really hard to hear what my turds were talking about.

The internet is a dangerous place to let kids explore unsupervised. If you want your kids to have independence, tell them that it's a parent's responsibility to register their kids for every site they're allowed to use. If a child checks out a website that they're not registered for, the police will come a-calling.

HOW TO AVOID THEM USING YOUR CREDIT CARD

Everyone knows that the card number on a credit card contains the nuclear launch codes. If it's not input correctly, with the non-warfare PIN, then it triggers a red alert at a secret military base, and the president is notified of an imminent launch. Obviously.

I never tried smoking as a teenager, because when I was about eight, my parents got an old guy they knew to pretend to be a 25-year-old smoker version of me who had traveled from the future to tell me never to start. I was haunted by this haggard version of myself for years!

When kids "run away," it's usually just to the end of the street to get attention. But if you want to avoid the fuss of acting worried and then being "relieved" when they turn up, tell your adventurous young adults that if they ever left, you would have to move immediately, because you wouldn't be able to bear being there without them, and they'd have no way of tracking you down again—which would be a shame.

HA HA HA

HOW TO GET THEM TO SIT UP STRAIGHT

While there are more important things than perfect posture, put your offspring off slouching by telling them that the more they slouch, the quicker they will devolve into a monkey. Show them the "evolution of man" drawing in reverse to really have them hooked on straight-up sitting.

Put them off putting their fingers in their mouth by telling them that human nails are particularly calorific. Professional endurance athletes usually snack on them during races to keep them energized. Therefore, the more they bite them, the fewer cookies they'll be allowed to eat to counteract all their human-nail feasting.

> I had a fear of farting on the plane when I was a child because my parents told me that it affects the air pressure and can cause the plane to crash. They told me that the locks on the toilet doors had a special seal that meant you could fart in there without a fear of certain death.

Keep sticky fingerprints away from your important documents by stressing the secretive nature of your work. Sure, you might look like a [insert job here], but you're actually a secret agent, and those files and piles of paper are covered in vital clues and uncracked codes. It's imperative, for the country's safety, that they are kept in order.

HOW TO AVOID MICROWAVE MISHAPS

We know not to put metal in the microwave, but kids often have to learn these things by trial and error—error being a broken microwave and a big ol' mess in *your* kitchen. Luckily, adults know that if you *do* put metal in the microwave the electromagnetic radiation charges the earth's core. If it receives too many signals at once (from too many kids putting metal in the microwave), the earth will implode in an instant.

HA HA HA

We begged my parents for beanbags for years because our neighbors had them. Mom told us that she didn't believe in buying beanbags because they were filled with ground-up pieces of naughty children's bones.

HOW TO KEEP THEM UNDER CONTROL AT THE MOVIES

The big-screen experience is exciting, but lots of kids forget that they're not at home in their living room. Tell them that talking loudly, getting up to go to the toilet multiple times and throwing popcorn are all offenses you'll get kicked out for—but to avoid disturbing other movie-goers, your seat will simply fall away into a big underground rubbish tip for the remainder of the film.

Learning basic gratitude and polite behavior is important, especially if you don't want your kids to show you up. Introduce the idea of the Polite Pixie, a friendly imp who feels pain every time children are rude. When you say please and thank you, she sprinkles invisible glitter onto your head so all the other pixies know to take good care of you.

HOW TO HANDLE THE DEATH OF A PET

The thought of Rex running off into the sunset to play on a fictional farm for retired dogs won't appease all kids. For the more skeptical, tell them that the law states old dogs must go to live at retirement homes to keep older people company.

Once we were at the hardware store and I was messing around. My dad told me that if I didn't do as I was told, he would trade me in for another kid that looked just like me at the Kid Store, and that I would be broken down for parts.

Of course, you LOVE everything your child draws and makes at school, but your fridge is only big enough to display a few choice pieces and there's only so many macaroni portraits anyone needs. If you've thrown away a bit of their work and they ask where it is, tell them that a neighbor was over and offered to buy it, so you sold it and put the money into their university fund.

HA HA HA

HOW TO MAKE THE BABYSITTER'S LIFE EASIER

Kids can make a babysitter's day a nightmare. Make sure your angels sit quietly on the sofa until you return by telling them that you don't trust the babysitter. You think they might be a CIA operative embedded in your house. Tell them to keep quiet, listen closely to anything they say for clues, and keep an eye on them at all times (unless they go to the toilet) to make sure they don't plant any secret devices.

I told my daughter that when she was born, the hospital gave me a unique parenting manual just for her. When she would ask to do something I didn't want her to do or wanted to eat something I didn't want her to eat, I would tell her, "Sorry, it says you're not allowed that in the manual."

If your animal-loving mini person is pestering you for a rabbit, tell them that rabbits were originally bred during the Cold War, and were trained as Soviet spies to tunnel under important government buildings, bringing them down from the inside. While they might look cute, their natural instincts are to destroy everything in their path.

HOW TO KEEP TECH AWAY FROM THE DINNER TABLE

Family dinners can be few and far between with busy lives. Keep all gadgets out of sight when you sit down for supper by explaining to the kids that nanotechnology in their tablets or phones interferes with human digestive systems. Every time they receive a notification, a small signal alerts the stomach that a robot is nearby, causing it to momentarily shut down and giving them a stomach ache as a result. It's science, obviously.

HOW TO KEEP NEW THINGS LOOKING NICE

When you buy a brand-new sofa or a solid-oak dining set, you want it to stay nice for as long as possible, which can be hard with sticky hands and boisterous playtimes. Explain to the kids that the shop is just being nice and lending the furniture to you, and that if they damage it, scary men will come and take it away again and you'll all have to sit on the floor.

HA HA HA

To help my children fall back to sleep when they were sick, I would give them some medicine and tell them that it said on the instructions that it would only work if the unwell child fell asleep in their own bed straight after taking it. They would get back into bed immediately and close their eyes without complaint.

Going to the dentist is an unpleasant experience at the best of times, but to make sure your kids don't suffer from dentophobia, remind them that the dentist is actually mining for gold. They need to check your teeth to make sure there's no treasure lurking inside there that the tooth fairy could steal for herself. If they find any, they split the profits with you 50/50.

HOW TO CLEAN UP CUTS AND SCRAPES

Getting cuts and bruises is all part of growing up, but some kids are more upset about the disinfectant you want to rub on their knee than the wound itself. Tell them it's vampire repellent, and that if you don't put it on, vampires will be able to smell their blood and will come and find them during the night.

If your children are scared of goblins, ghouls or vampires, tell them that in the 1950s all the monsters moved to Hollywood to make their names in the movies and never bothered to leave. If you live in Hollywood, say they moved to New York to be on Broadway instead!

At my house the tooth fairy is a real jet-setter. When I forgot to leave money under my kids' pillows, I told them it was because she had a late pick-up in Brazil and was currently crossing the Atlantic, but that she would show up the next night once she'd got back.

HOW TO GET THEM TO APPRECIATE THE LITTLE THINGS

Make small change more appealing by telling kids that every year the mint makes a few special coins of low value that they put out with the rest of the money (make up something they have to check for). A bit like in *Charlie and the Chocolate Factory*, if they find the special coin, they'll win something amazing— more money, perhaps? That's why, when you give them small coins as pocket money, you're being super-generous.

HOW TO GET THEM TO WASH THEIR HANDS BEFORE THEY EAT

Washing your hands before you eat is a healthy habit for kids to get into. If they think germs have tiny feet that will walk them down a fork and into their food, even better. Explain how some germs are so daring, they will sit on their bums and slide down the metal shaft right onto their favorite food, just waiting to be gobbled up.

A simple trick to make sure your kids are truth tellers is to ask them something you know they'll lie about: "Did you eat the last cookie?" and then say, "Let me hold your thumbs," as if that's a completely normal way for adults to assess if the truth is being told. Pretend to discern their lies through the pulse in the thumbs and they'll be a lot more honest in future.

"

Nowadays there's an app for everything. I exploit this to great effect with my kids. I told them there's an app that knows if they've brushed their teeth and for how long, to make sure they brush properly. I also had an app at one point that told me when they got out of bed in the night.

"

Bribery is great, but this convincing lie might just have them reaching for the math book as bedtime reading. Tell them that all adults have to take times-table tests every year and if they fail, they'll have to go back to school until they improve. If they don't learn their times tables now, they'll be screwed when they grow up. Show them a number or letter on your passport or driving licence that proves you've passed or shows your score.

HA HA HA

HOW TO CONVINCE THEM THE TOY SHOP IS CLOSED

Before they're old enough to read the "open" sign, you can tell your kids that the toy shop is closed, even when it's open. If they ask why the lights are still on, you can say, "They leave the lights on for the toys so they don't get scared while the shopkeeper is away."

HA HA HA

HOW TO GET THEM TO GROW THEIR HAIR

If you're obsessed with long, luscious locks and want to live vicariously through your kids, tell them that haircuts are really painful. When you brush their hair and they wince and whine at the pain of getting out a tangle, tell them that that's nothing compared to a haircut. You'll get to keep their hair long and save money on cuts for years.

We don't have a fireplace or a chimney in our house, so I told my kids that when Santa came to visit, he liquefied and came in through the pipes. It terrified my youngest son. One Christmas Eve he went round the house blocking up the taps and plugholes with toilet paper to stop "Evil Santa" from getting in.

Want your tree to look fancy all festive season long? Tell your kids it contains the spirit of Christmas and that each time they touch it or poke the ornaments, they take away some of its magical power. And we all know what happens if the magic goes—Santa won't be able to find their house.

HOW TO STOP THEM SWALLOWING GUM

For years, the thought of rotting gum in your stomach was enough to put off lots of little ones from gobbling it down (either on purpose or by mistake), but that warning might not be enough to deter today's postmillennial minors. So, if they're prone to swallowing, tell them it will turn their teeth blue and make their hair sticky.

HOW TO HANDLE SENSITIVE MATERIAL

If your kids stumble across something they're not supposed to (either from your own collection of analogue "adult material" or while browsing for *Paw Patrol* on the computer), don't terrorize them with the truth too soon. Tell them that they are medical textbooks/videos/memes that you're studying so you can become a doctor when you're older.

HA HA HA

My brother, sister and I used to always fight over who got to sit in the front seat. Our dad told us that the reason it's called "shotgun" was because it was the seat where you had to operate the car's built-in gun in emergency situations. Ergo, only adults were allowed to sit up front. He happily chauffeured us around for years, the three of us squished in the back.

HOW TO SCARE THEM INTO USING THE TOILET

Potty training is HARD WORK. If the usual positive approach is failing you, tell your little ones about the potty monster. Tell them that if they don't start using the toilet by [insert appropriate date here], then the potty monster will start throwing their poop back at them or, heaven forbid, pull them down into the depths of potty land.

HOW TO HELP THEM LOVE THEMSELVES JUST THE WAY THEY ARE

Kids these days are more obsessed with appearance than ever before. Instill a sense of personal pride and self-confidence in yours. Tell them that if they don't learn to appreciate their wonky eyes, frizzy hair or big nose, then when they reach puberty all the parts of their body that they dislike will fall off, and you'll have to buy them an eyepatch, wig or rubber nose.

> I didn't go to the zoo until it was part of a school trip when I was ten. My mom couldn't afford it, so she told us the pet store was the zoo. We used to spend ages looking at the rabbits, guinea pigs and turtles none the wiser.

HOW TO MAKE SURE THEY EAT BREAKFAST

Make your morning routine a breeze by convincing your kids that breakfast really is the most important meal of the day—it forms a soft landing in their stomach for the rest of the food to follow. If they don't eat it up, their stomachs won't be prepped for snack time, lunch or dinner, and they won't be able to eat another bite until the next morning.

Veggies aren't always the most exciting choices for pizza-mad little ones, but tell them that if they don't eat enough colorful foods from nature then all the colors will disappear and the world will go back to being black and white, like in the olden days when people just ate potatoes. Show them old black-and-white photos to convince them.

HA HA HA HA